COMMUNION

I0516922

COMMUNION
CHURCHLEADERS
PASTORAL POCKET GUIDES

First Edition: Year 2022
Communion (ChurchLeaders Pastoral Pocket Guides) / Outreach, Inc.
Paperback ISBN: 978-1-958585-00-9
eBook ISBN: 978-1-958585-01-6

CHURCHLEADERS
PRESS

Colorado Springs

CHURCHLEADERS
PASTORAL POCKET GUIDES

COMMUNION

Written by
Mark A. Taylor

General Editor
Matt Lockhart

CHURCHLEADERS
PRESS

Colorado Springs

Contents

ChurchLeaders
Pastoral Pocket Guides Introduction

Be shepherds of God's flock that is under your care, watching over them—not because you must, but because you are willing, as God wants you to be; not pursuing dishonest gain, but eager to serve; not lording it over those entrusted to you, but being examples to the flock.
(1 Peter 5:2-3)

*T*he work of a shepherd is never done. One minute you're preparing a sermon and the next you're making an emergency hospital visit or planning an unexpected funeral.

When called to your common and recurring ministerial duties (such as hospital visits, weddings, baptisms, and funerals, to name a few) where do you turn for practical advice or just a couple fresh ideas?

You could spend hours online, scrolling through dozens of sites, or pull that thick, old minister's manual off your shelf. Now you can turn to these new **Pastoral Pocket Guides**, designed especially for busy pastors like you. They're quick reads, each book laser-focused on a specific area of ministry. Packed with practical guidance, tips, and tools, they'll help make taking care of your flock a little easier.

Thank you for being a willing shepherd. May God bless and guide you in your ministry!

—**Matthew Lockhart,** General Editor

1 WELCOME TO THE COMMUNION POCKET GUIDE

*W*hether you're a pastor, worship leader, elder, or volunteer on the church's Communion team, you'll find help in this pocket guide. If you are an experienced leader, leaf through these pages to gain new ideas for Communion times. If you're new at presiding at the Lord's Table, you'll find more than enough here to get yourself started well.

The book begins with a biblical look at Communion to refresh your thinking about why this observation is important and what it means to those who participate in it.

It also provides guidelines for meaningful Communion services. Even if you've been presiding over Communion for years, you may find something fresh to consider here.

The bulk of this handy guide gives possibilities for what to say and how to pray at Communion. Find here sample Communion meditations, Scriptures to use with Communion, meditation prompts, possibilities for particular occasions, and extended services for a retreat or special service.

Perhaps the greatest value to you will be prods and possibilities for lifting Communion from the routine to the refreshing. Just as daily physical meals are enriched by some new or surprising element, Communion for you and your church can offer deeper renewal as leaders like you give it special thought.

2 IN REMEMBERING, WE'RE RENEWED

*C*ommunion, the Lord's Supper, the Eucharist. Christians have used various words for the practice that is the focus of this pocket guide. All the terms have biblical roots and are used to describe a longstanding Christian rite.[1] While not every denomination shares the same theology related to this observance, the Church at large agrees that we should observe Communion. This pocket guide aims to help this happen thoughtfully, creatively, and in a way that inspires meaningful worship.

But before delving into ways to honor God and engage believers with this observance, we do well to stop and ask ourselves why observe it at all. We have seen Christians in every kind of church group making Communion a significant part of their worship. Why is it important to follow their example here? The Bible suggests several answers:

A foundation
Jesus instituted the Lord's Supper at his last meal with his disciples, the Passover observance that happened

---

1   https://www.crosswalk.com/faith/bible-study/10-things-you-should-know-about-the-lord-s-supper-from-1-corinthians.html

just before his arrest and crucifixion. Since the time of Moses, Jews had celebrated Passover to remember how God saved their firstborn sons from death in the plague that befell the Egyptians. Following God's orders for this first Passover, the Israelites took blood from a sacrificed lamb and wiped it on the doorframe of every one of their homes. When the Lord came through the land claiming the Egyptian sons, the Israelite families were spared (Exodus 12).

Likewise, Christ, the Lamb of God (John 1:29) was sacrificed centuries later to protect all his followers from the eternal death caused by sin. His death established a new covenant between God and all who would know him (Matthew 26:27-28).

Communion symbolizes a bedrock of our faith, this death of Christ to spare us the punishment for our sins.

A remembrance

Jesus left his disciples with a command that Christians ever since have obeyed: "Do this . . . in remembrance of me" (1 Corinthians 11:25).

Jesus wants us never to forget what he gave, which is why we worship him. Communion keeps our focus on the center of our faith. It helps us remember the sacrifice that sustains our hope and strengthens our faith.

A memorial

Christ gave us physical symbols, the cup and the loaf, to engage all our senses in the remembering. The taste of the fruit of the vine in our mouths reminds us of the blood that poured from Christ's wounds at Calvary. The broken bread is a picture of his broken body.

Jesus knew that something to hold and see would help us keep straight the facts of his sacrifice. Like a statue in the city square helps us remember war heroes or a founding father, like a bracelet or ring helps us remember someone we love, these simple physical symbols are tangible reminders of what Christ did for us.

A celebration

Observing Communion was central in the worship of the first church. The believers "devoted themselves to the apostles' teaching and the fellowship, to the breaking of bread and the prayers" (Acts 2:42). At first, they made the observance a part of their regular fellowship meal (1 Corinthians 11:17-33). Later they kept the observance without the meal, and eventually, early Christians celebrated Communion daily.[2]

---

2   For a fuller history see "Eucharist" at https://www. britannica.com/topic/Eucharist

Although that practice has disappeared in many circles, we continue the practice of all Christians in all times with our regular observance of the Lord's Supper. It is the celebration that distinguishes us as followers of Christ.

A self-examination

At Communion, we ponder the reality of our own sins. Lest we somehow fool ourselves into believing we don't need the salvation that comes only from Jesus, observing Communion reminds us otherwise. "Everyone ought to examine themselves before they eat of the bread and drink from the cup," Paul told the church at Corinth (1 Corinthians 11:28).

A warning

In this same passage, Paul seems to have a double meaning when he says, "Those who eat and drink without discerning the body of Christ eat and drink judgment on themselves" (v. 29). Obviously, this means our Communion observance should not be flippant, self-centered, or rushed.

But in this passage, Paul was also condemning the Corinthian church for excluding some poorer Christians from their fellowship meal. Some ate and drank to excess while others were left out. He seems to be saying in verse 29 that the church today is also the body of Christ. When we come to Communion nurturing divisions among Christians, we are not properly discerning this.

An expression of unity

In a broader sense, many believers have found in Communion an act of worship that can be celebrated among Christians with widely varying views on many theological or practical issues. Those with varying understandings of the Holy Spirit's activity or the role of women in leadership, those with formal worship and those praising God with guitars and drums, those whose pastors wear robes, and those with pastors in jeans and tennis shoes—all these and a dozen other differences fade to the background when we focus together on the cross of Jesus and the sacrifice that saves us.

Even in a local congregation experiencing division or conflict over one issue or another, we can lift up Communion as an observance that reminds us of what we have in common. "We are one body" (1 Corinthians 10:17) remembering Jesus.

A proclamation

Paul told the Corinthians (1 Corinthians 11:26), "whenever you eat this bread and drink this cup, you proclaim the Lord's death until he comes." This is the message that sustains us in our service, in our disappointments, in our suffering. This is the message that has the potential to offer hope and meaning to spiritual wanderers in the world all around us. In Communion, we lift up the distinctive that makes Christianity worth living and dying for. And so we continue to observe Communion because the cross of our risen Lord compels all men and women through all time to awestruck wonder and life-changing worship.

3 COMMUNION TODAY

Some words, practices, or traditions wear well with repetition. Little children look forward to the Christmas story read by Grandpa every Christmas Eve. Families anticipate dinner together on birthdays or holidays. Husbands send the same flowers to their wives every anniversary. And no matter how many times someone says the words, we never tire of hearing, "I love you."

But sometimes the repetition comes without thought, without remembering why the words or traditions are important, or without savoring the significance and relishing the experience we have shared so often. And so we let the oldest child read the Christmas story as a special treat. We take the family dinner to a park or an expensive restaurant. The husband encloses a special message or surprise gift with the bouquet. We put "I love you" in a lunchbox note or a social media post, or tell this person in public why we love him or her so much.

There's nothing wrong with repeating similar words or going through a familiar routine with each celebration of Communion. Indeed, with the Lord's introduction of the practice, he used common elements that were staples of every meal.

The ideas in this chapter are not meant to make us feel inferior if our Communion services follow a familiar pattern. There's no attempt here to *add* meaning where it already exists, only to *rekindle* emotion and *stimulate* thought about what we're doing and why, when we partake.

If your church leaders or denominational practices stipulate a formula for your Communion services, of course you'll follow it. But if you have the freedom to enjoy some variety or inject some creativity, please do so. Even small fresh touches can catch the attention and engage the thinking of worshippers in ways that will bring all of you closer to God.

Here are a few ideas:

To remember as you plan

Prepare your heart. Even though all the above is true, it comes with a caveat. The Communion planner must evaluate himself with each plan he makes. Communion is a time to focus on Christ and his sacrifice, not an opportunity to get attention for the worship leader. Our goal is to serve, not to impress. This whole pocket guide has been written amid prayers that God would use it to lead the church to celebrate Communion in a way that honors Christ and glorifies God. When that prayer precedes each plan for a Communion service, both the leader and the worshipper will be moved anew with the meaning at the root of your observance.

Focus on the cross. Many congregations precede each Communion service with a meditation like some of those suggested in this guide. Some newcomers, or even experienced pastors, tend to forget what their meditation should accomplish. The point of whatever someone says before Communion is to remind worshippers again of the singular act of sacrifice Jesus gave and the essential function it performed.

This is not a time for a general devotion or inspirational thought. A creative approach may be good; a tie-in with the calendar or current events can help. But the landing place must always be Calvary. Jesus said to remember his broken body and his shed blood. If we cannot find a new way to say that, it's better to repeat what we've heard before than to sidestep the cross altogether in an effort to be original. This is not a sermon or homily about just anything the Bible addresses. Here our mandate from Jesus himself is, "Remember me."

Ideas for your plan

Connect it with what comes before and after. Try to avoid the tendency for Communion to feel like a necessary interruption. The worship song shared just before the Communion service will probably contain a phrase or idea that can be the first thought in the Communion meditation. Help worshippers connect with a stream of thought or challenge instead of forcing them to start over now that it's Communion time.

Vary the placement in the service. Some churches always place Communion after the singing and before the offering and sermon. God does not require you to put it there.

Some churches always place Communion at the end of the service, like a coda that's necessary to complete before dismissal. Could a different placement, at least from time to time, help worshippers rethink what Communion is all about?

Maybe Communion could help worshippers focus on one point in the sermon, and you would interrupt the sermon with the Communion service. Maybe Communion could be a time for every worshipper to respond to the challenge just delivered in the sermon, and the Communion service could be cast as a time of decision for all. Maybe the whole service now and then could focus on the cross and include partaking of the Communion elements. Maybe participants would partake of the broken loaf at one point in the service and the fruit of the vine at another, with meditations or music in between.

Vary the leaders. Ask women, teenagers, or children to read Scriptures surrounding the service. Recruit a few members ahead of time to stand where they're sitting or come to the front to read or pray. Invite a husband-and-wife team to prepare a brief reading and incorporate it into your service. Assemble a diverse group of church members to come to the front and instruct them ahead of time each to offer a simple one-sentence prayer to precede partaking of the emblems.

Choose leaders whose gift is presentation. Not every pastor or elder or other church officer has the ability to engage a crowd from the platform, and that's OK. Use those who have been gifted by God to serve in this way, regardless of their place in your church governance.

Consider who passes the elements for Communion. Use family teams (dads and sons, mothers and daughters, or whole families) to pass the elements. Teenagers could do this one Sunday. Senior citizens could do this another week.

Make time. At least now and then, give five extra minutes for Communion, even if this means asking the pastor to preach that much shorter or the worship leader to transfer some of the general singing to this service.

Avoid the tendency to make Communion feel like a cursory requirement, like the forms you sign before surgery or the membership card you show the gatekeeper at Costco or Sam's Club. Communion is the main event. Communion is not the only reason we worship, but it is the single element Jesus specified for our worship.

A word about children. Encourage parents to involve their children in the Communion observance as appropriate. Congregations have different expectations for who will partake, ranging all the way from "open communion" to "for church members only."

Whatever the policy is in your congregation, from time to time, explain it clearly and involve your children's ministry in teaching about Communion.

Suggest also that parents talk with their children about the meaning of Communion. Here's one example to help equip parents in talking with their kids: "Jesus and his disciples drank something like what we drink and ate bread like we use in our Communion service. He told them the drink should remind them of his blood shed at Calvary. The bread reminds us of his body. We thank God for the love of Jesus when we take Communion."

Rise above rote

Sometimes at home, we repeat "I love you" as a simple habit as we walk out the door or our children leave for school. There's nothing wrong with that. But sometimes, we need to sit face-to-face with our child or our spouse or our parent and find a way to tell them how much our love for them means to us.

Like all traditions, "I love you" can lose its meaning with repetition. Like all traditions, Communion can be rote without some special attention. Every leader has the opportunity with each service he plans to make sure that doesn't happen.

4 SCRIPTURES AND COMMUNION MEDITATION PROMPTS

A few sentences under each of these Scriptures can guide your thoughts as you prepare a Communion meditation as part of a regular worship service. At the end of this chapter, find Scriptures and thoughts for special situations.

John 19:19

Pilate had a notice prepared and fastened to the cross. It read: JESUS OF NAZARETH, THE KING OF THE JEWS.

We can't be sure of Pilate's motivation for the sign he put on the cross of Jesus, but we can affirm the title was accurate. Jesus is King, not only of the Jews but for all men and women for all time. By his death and resurrection, he proved he is the one who deserves that title.

Romans 3:21-24 and 5:8

But now apart from the law the righteousness of God has been made known, to which the Law and the Prophets testify. This righteousness is given through faith in Jesus Christ to all who believe. There is no difference between Jew and Gentile, for all have sinned and fall short of the glory of God, and all are justified freely by his grace through the redemption that came by Christ Jesus.

But God demonstrates his own love for us in this: While we were still sinners, Christ died for us.

He did not wait for us to be "good enough." He does not expect us to "earn" our love from God because he knew that is not possible. He did what only he could do to provide what really matters.

Romans 3:25-26

God presented Christ as a sacrifice of atonement, through the shedding of his blood—to be received by faith. He did this to demonstrate his righteousness, because in his forbearance he had left the sins committed beforehand unpunished—he did it to demonstrate his righteousness at the present time, so as to be just and the one who justifies those who have faith in Jesus.

"Atonement" is a theological description of a simply beautiful idea. Through Christ's sacrifice, we can be at one with God. Can we imagine any other relationship that could matter more?

1 Corinthians 1:18-25

For the message of the cross is foolishness to those who are perishing, but to us who are being saved it is the power of God. For it is written:

"I will destroy the wisdom of the wise; the intelligence of the intelligent I will frustrate."

Where is the wise person? Where is the teacher of the law? Where is the philosopher of this age? Has not God made foolish the wisdom of the world? For since in the wisdom of God the world through its wisdom did not know him, God was pleased through the foolishness of what was preached to save those who believe. Jews demand signs and Greeks look for wisdom, but we preach Christ crucified: a stumbling block to Jews and foolishness to Gentiles, but to those whom God has called, both Jews and Greeks, Christ the power of God and the wisdom of God. For the foolishness of God is wiser than human wisdom, and the weakness of God is stronger than human strength.

What we remember today is as central as it seems senseless to a world without God. But our steadfast observance of this meal is a testimony as well as a reminder that Christ's sacrifice is our only path to hope and purpose and salvation.

1 Corinthians 10:16-17

Is not the cup of thanksgiving for which we give thanks a participation in the blood of Christ? And is not the bread that we break a participation in the body of Christ? Because there is one loaf, we, who are many, are one body, for we all share the one loaf.

One bread, one body; one sacrifice, and one church. Christ's death sets the stage for unity the world seeks but can never accomplish without him.

Galatians 2:20

I have been crucified with Christ and I no longer live, but Christ lives in me. The life I now live in the body, I live by faith in the Son of God, who loved me and gave himself for me.

This is a time for resolve as well as remembrance. Christ's crucifixion is not only the means by which we can be saved but also the example we must learn to follow.

Galatians 6:14

May I never boast except in the cross of our Lord Jesus Christ, through which the world has been crucified to me, and I to the world.

Any of us may give our lifetimes to building a reputation around the values we cherish most. At the Lord's Table, we are reminded of what must top that list: we are saved by and dedicated to the power in the cross to give life true meaning.

Ephesians 1:7-10

In him we have redemption through his blood, the forgiveness of sins, in accordance with the riches of God's grace that he lavished on us. With all wisdom and understanding, he made known to us the mystery of his will according to his good pleasure, which he purposed in Christ, to be put into effect when the times reach their fulfillment—to bring unity to all things in heaven and on earth under Christ.

His blood flowed freely in a spectacle of suffering too horrible to see without wincing. But it was the means of the grace from God that comes in a lavish flow too wonderful to ignore.

Colossians 1:15-20

The Son is the image of the invisible God, the firstborn over all creation. For in him all things were created: things in heaven and on earth, visible and invisible, whether thrones or powers or rulers or authorities; all things have been created through him and for him. He is before all things, and in him all things hold together. And he is the head of the body, the church; he is the beginning and the firstborn from among the dead, so that in everything he might have the supremacy. For God was pleased to have all his fullness dwell in him, and through him to reconcile to himself all things, whether things on earth or things in heaven, by making peace through his blood, shed on the cross.

All things are held together by the one whose death allows all things and every person to be reconciled to God. Today we remember a sacrifice, but much more. We realize we worship the one whose sacrifice is central to the very existence and hope of the whole world.

Titus 2:11-14

For the grace of God has appeared that offers salvation to all people. It teaches us to say "No" to ungodliness and worldly passions, and to live self-controlled, upright and godly lives in this present age, while we wait for the blessed hope—the appearing of the glory of our great God and Savior, Jesus Christ, who gave himself for us to redeem us from all wickedness and to purify for himself a people that are his very own, eager to do what is good.

We think about ourselves at Communion, and we should. But that's not all. The apostle tells us God's goal was to "purify for himself a people that are his very own, eager to do what is good." Let us commit ourselves in this moment to finding ways as a church to "do good" in our day and in our community.

Hebrews 9:27-28

Just as people are destined to die once, and after that to face judgment, so Christ was sacrificed once to take away the sins of many; and he will appear a second time, not to bear sin, but to bring salvation to those who are waiting for him.

As surrounded as we are by all the evils of this world, it is hard to imagine the doing away of all sin. But as we remember Christ's sacrifice centuries ago, we anticipate his promise that gives us hope for a future without the scars and suffering of sin.

1 Peter 1:18-19

For you know that it was not with perishable things such as silver or gold that you were redeemed from the empty way of life handed down to you from your ancestors, but with the precious blood of Christ, a lamb without blemish or defect.

In our affluence, we see people all around us trying to purchase peace or satisfaction or joy. But God did not use temporary treasures of this world to achieve eternal peace in our lives. The "precious blood of Christ" makes this possible.

1 John 1:6-7

If we claim to have fellowship with him and yet walk in the darkness, we lie and do not live out the truth. But if we walk in the light, as he is in the light, we have fellowship with one another, and the blood of Jesus, his Son, purifies us from all sin.

In this observance of Communion, we step into the light of God's reality, and we celebrate the joy of our salvation.

Revelation 4:8

Each of the four living creatures had six wings and was covered with eyes all around, even under its wings. Day and night they never stop saying:

> *"'Holy, holy, holy*
> *is the Lord God Almighty,'*
> *who was, and is, and is to come."*

We are not remembering the sacrifice of some historical hero whose accomplishment brings temporary good. Here we focus on Christ, whose death has created a kingdom that will last forever.

5 FOUR COMMUNION MEDITATIONS TO USE ANY TIME

Past, Present, and Future

*O*ften at Communion, we read the record of Jesus setting the precedent for Communion at the Passover feast he observed with his disciples just before his death (Luke 22:17-20). And in that account, we see the significance of this event in the past, for the present, and for the future.

Jesus spoke to the disciples, in words they did not yet understand, about the event we remember today. When he mentioned his "body given for you" and "my blood, which is poured out for you," he was describing his own crucifixion. Following his lead, we use simple bread and fruit of the vine to symbolize his broken body and shed blood, and we commemorate the event from history that set the stage for our worship today.

Jesus commanded the disciples to "do this in remembrance of me," which is why we include this symbolic meal at the center of our worship today. Jesus gave a command that is the catalyst for worship week after week after week all around the world.

But as we celebrate, we are not simply remembering a heroic sacrifice from the past. Jesus spoke of drinking the fruit of the vine when "the kingdom of God comes." He labeled the cup as the "new covenant in my blood." We look to the future as we partake of these emblems because by Christ's sacrifice, we have the hope of seeing the answer to the petition in his model prayer: "Your kingdom come, your will be done, on earth as it is in heaven" (Matthew 6:10).

For all times, in all places, among all peoples, Jesus died. We thank him, we remember him, we praise him, we anticipate a grand reunion someday at a time we don't know and in a place we can't see. This is why we celebrate Communion today.

No Secrets

*D*id you ever do something wrong and keep it a secret?

Maybe your mom blamed your brother for cutting into the cake she was saving for company, but you're the one who had tasted it ahead of time.

Maybe you got together with some buddies to pull off a senior-year prank, and they never did find out who sank the statue in the school swimming pool.

Maybe you bumped a car in a parking lot and drove off without leaving a note.

Or maybe your secret is something far more serious, and you still have succeeded in not letting anyone find out about your indiscretion, infidelity, or dishonesty.

If so, how does that feel? I'm guessing you can relate to the psalmist's words. He said, "When I kept silent, my bones wasted away through my groaning all day long. For day and night your hand was heavy on me; my strength was sapped as in the heat of summer" (Psalm 32:3-4). Or maybe you've had the glorious experience of coming clean with your mom or your insurance company or your boss or your spouse. Hopefully, all of us have come clean with God. Hopefully, all of us can echo the psalmist's experience as he recounts it in the next verse. "Then I acknowledged my sin to you," he says in his prayer, "and did not cover up my iniquity. I said, 'I will confess my transgressions to the Lord.' And you forgave the guilt of my sin" (v. 5).

We know this morning that forgiveness is made possible by the sacrifice of Jesus on the cross of Calvary. The Scripture says, "The blood of Jesus . . . purifies us from all sin" (1 John 1:7).

God already knows about our sin. By acknowledging it to him, we come closer to him and prepare ourselves to live with joy and peace. As we pray this morning, confess and celebrate what Jesus did that makes that confession full of potential.

The Beauty of Balance

*I*n all of life, balance is an elusive goal. The supervisor praises workers but holds them accountable to certain standards for performance. The generous parent loves to please his children with gifts, but he knows he must teach them the value of working toward their goals. Busy executives, schoolteachers, or doctors are committed to their work, but they know they will not be effective if they don't regularly leave work for rest.

As we come to Communion, we may fall into one of two inadequate extremes.

Some consider Christianity and are overwhelmed by how far they fall short of an exemplary moral life. "I could never be good enough for church. I'm really not a good person, and those who don't know it would certainly kick me out once they found out how bad I really am."

Others look around and decide they're pretty good compared to the average. "Yeah, my favorite TV show is a little racy, but I'm not looking at the pornography those guys at work seem to enjoy." Or "Sure, I didn't report the income from my freelance gigs, but have you heard how all those billionaires get out of their taxes?"

Most of us have known someone who said either, "I'm too terrible" or "I'm good enough." But the message of the cross pulls us back from either extreme.

The Bible makes it clear, "All have sinned and fall short of the glory of God" (Romans 3:23). Elsewhere in the letter containing that quote, the apostle Paul makes it clear that even one small infraction of the law makes a man as guilty as if he had committed first-degree murder.

But Scripture also reminds us that "The Lord . . . is patient with you, not wanting anyone to perish, but everyone to come to repentance" (2 Peter 3:9). "God so loved the world that he gave his one and only Son, that whoever believes in him shall not perish but have eternal life" (John 3:16).

In that "whoever," we find balance. The most debauched degenerate and the most respected saint find common ground at the foot of the cross. Here, as we remember Christ's broken body and sacrificed blood, we find balance. And in this balance, we discover the only way to live with joy and peace. This is why we celebrate Communion.

Lord, Please Heal!

*H*ealthcare spending in the United States in 2021 was about $4.3 trillion![3] Even if we didn't realize it before, that figure alone would show us that health is a major concern for all of us. Young people worshipping with us this morning may be rather laid-back about their health. But by middle age, most of us are visiting the doctor, updating our prescriptions, and comparing our aches and pains with anyone who will listen.

Physical health can become a consuming concern as age advances, but spiritual health is a problem for every generation. The Bible makes a connection between physical and spiritual health, but even if we're feeling fine, we need the spiritual checkup provided by our meeting at the Lord's Table.

It's intriguing to think about Scripture's promise to heal and to see how that healing springs from the sacrifice of Jesus on the cross.

The prophet Isaiah was looking ahead to Jesus when he said, "He was pierced for our transgressions, he was crushed for our iniquities; the punishment that brought us peace was on him, and by his wounds we are healed (Isaiah 53:5). Later the apostle Peter looked back at Calvary and quoted the same words in the letter we

---

3   https://www.wsj.com/articles/u-s-healthcare-spending-slowed-in-2021-after-covid-19-surge-11648497601

know as 1 Peter: "He himself bore our sins in his body on the cross," Peter wrote, "so that we might die to sins and live for righteousness" (1 Peter 2:24).

Peter also quoted Isaiah by including the prophet's assessment of whether physical health should be our primary concern:

> *"All people are like grass, and all their glory is like the flowers of the field; the grass withers and the flowers fail, but the word of the Lord endures forever"* (1 Peter 1:24-25).

Some of us realize we are worshipping today with failing bodies. The fact is that none of our bodies will last forever. But our hope beyond death comes from Jesus, who lived beyond the grave. We know we will be healed by his precious blood. And we celebrate today because that sacrifice addresses not only an eternal future but also speaks to the emotional, psychological, or spiritual sickness he also wants to heal in the here and now.

As we prepare to remember Christ's healing sacrifice, let us pray this morning with the psalmist:

> *"Have mercy on me, Lord, for I am faint; heal me, Lord, for my bones are in agony. My soul is in deep anguish" (Psalm 6:2-3). We realize,*

Lord, that you will provide for our bodies, and even more significantly, for our souls. Thank you, Lord, for the health that comes only from you, provided by the sacrifice of your Son at Calvary.

6 COMMUNION PRAYERS FOR EVERY SEASON

Autumn

Dear God,

We acknowledge that you are the giver of every good and perfect gift. And while we may thank you for so many of them, none stands higher on our list than the gift of Christ whose death on Calvary gives our lives focus and purpose and hope and joy. Thank you, God, oh thank you, for the gift of Jesus that we remember in this hour.

Amen

Heavenly Father,

Surrounded as we are by greed and pride and selfishness, we struggle to grasp the height and width and depth of all you gave, just because you love us. In this moment, when we remember again the selflessness of Christ at Calvary, the simplicity of his life on earth, and the eternity he has prepared for all of us who follow him, renew us with hope, refocus us with purpose, and sustain us with your love.

Amen

Winter

Heavenly Father,

Short days and dark nights threaten to depress or discourage some, but just now, we thank you for Jesus, the light of the world, whose light gives hope to everyone who believes in him. We thank you that his light was not quenched at Calvary but only briefly darkened as a prelude to the glorious brightness of his departure from the grave. We celebrate because his sacrifice ignites the bright light of our hope today.

Amen

Dear God,

We stumble to express what we know to be true, that your eternal Son took on the bonds of human flesh and experienced the pains of human suffering just so that we could someday inherit a spiritual body with joy for eternity. As

*we contemplate a fragile baby in the manger,
we remember our broken Savior and celebrate
your love for us.*

Amen

Dear God,

*All around us, we're hearing "Happy New Year,"
but frankly, so much about his new year isn't
happy or particularly new. We know the sin that
has plagued humankind since the beginning of
time still ruins relationships, upends lives, and
damages human enterprises all around us. We
thank you, Lord, for Jesus, whose sacrifice at
Calvary is the only source of peace and joy that
can last for eternity. We celebrate his suffering
because it gives us strength to face every new
day, every new week, every new year with the
hope that comes only in you and because of him.*

Amen

Heavenly Father,

*While all the world is celebrating love, we're
remembering a love beyond what the world*

on its own can produce. The blood red of the Valentine's Day cards in our mailboxes reminds us of the scarlet sacrifice of Jesus and the gift of our salvation that only his blood could purchase.

Amen

Spring

Dear God,

We remember Christ's prayer at Calvary, "Father, forgive them for they don't know what they're doing." Just now, as we remember his death on that cross, we pray the same prayer for ourselves. Our sin surprises us; it happens before we know it, or without our knowing it. Father, forgive us, even as we thank you for the assurance we have that our sins can be forgiven.

Amen

Heavenly Father,

It's certainly true, Lord, that we can face tomorrow because Jesus lives today. And while

*we celebrate the resurrection of Christ, we
know the sacrifice of Christ makes his empty
grave more significant than any other miracle.
We're so thankful to know both parts of the good
news, Lord, and we remember them with joy as
we partake today.*

Amen

Dear God,

*The passing of one season into another, year
after year after year, reminds us of your great
faithfulness, mercy, and love. We know your
love will not disappear like melting snow or
fading blossoms, and we thank you for the
testimony of Calvary that assures us you still
love us, whatever else may be changing around
us.*

Amen

Summer

Dear God,

*We're astounded at the miracle of life as flowers
and crops burst forth into magnificent blooms*

and plants laden with fruit, all from seeds the size of sand or a pebble. We know you are the source of all life, and that our eternal life is possible because Christ died and was buried to burst forth with the promise of abundant potential for all who make him Lord. As we remember his sacrifice, we reaffirm our desire to make him Lord. And we watch for spiritual fruit to be born from our lives because we have submitted to you.

Amen

Heavenly Father,

In a season of time off, trips away, and rest from the routine, we're so grateful that you never take a day off. We're thankful that Christ, once crucified and then raised and now ascended, sits on your right hand to intercede for us always. If we've looked away from you in our vacation days, we ask you to forgive us. You know we can't really forget Christ's sacrifice for us, and we thank you just now for sending him to save us.

Amen

7 GUIDELINES FOR COMMUNION IN DIFFERENT SETTINGS

*M*aybe you'll be asked to bring Communion to a friend in the hospital. Maybe you'll be asked to join a team taking Communion to homebound shut-ins. Maybe you'll visit nursing home residents with Communion.

Although the Lord's Supper service in any of these settings is much like that in any other, the differences suggest some special thought and preparation. Here are a few guidelines:

Check ahead of time

If you'll visit in someone's home, make sure they'll be available when you want to come. If you're going to a nursing home or hospital, double-check visiting hours and verify whether there are any rules for visitors. Occasionally the person you serve will have dietary requirements affecting the elements themselves: Is the person you're visiting diabetic? Gluten free? Can they easily swallow and chew? You might check with a family member to let them know you're coming and to learn about any special situations.

Gather supplies

Many congregations have home Communion kits with cups and containers for juice and unleavened crackers. Some churches use individual communion cup juice-and-cracker combinations every Sunday or for special situations. If nothing else, you can probably purchase a small container of grape juice and a box of matzo crackers at your grocery. Include a few paper napkins, and you'll be ready to go.

Pray for wisdom and guidance

Before leaving for your visit(s), pray for each person you'll see. Ask God to work through you to bring them the blessing they need. Ask the Holy Spirit to intercede between your words and their eyes and ears to do what is needed in the heart and soul of each person you're visiting.

Remind yourself of the circumstances surrounding the person you'll visit. Have they been homebound a long time? Are they in the hospital for something critical or something more routine? Do they have family close by? Is this the first time they've received Communion in this setting, or are they accustomed to regular visits from Communion callers? Thinking and praying about each particular situation will prepare you to minister effectively.

Observe standard protocols

Wash your hands before and after visiting a hospital room. If the person is bedfast, do not sit on the bed with him or her. Stand, if you must, beside their bed. But, if possible, sit with them as you serve the elements, read Scripture, and pray. Make sure, in any case, that they can see your face, hear your voice, and feel a connection with you.

Do not rush through your visit or, on the other hand, stay too long. Gauge the energy level of the person you're visiting so that your time together will encourage them without wearing them out. Plan on about 15 minutes, but this is just a guideline. If you know the person well, are used to longer visits with them, and your schedule allows, enjoy as much time together as both of you would like.

Experience and express the Body of Christ

Your brief Communion service is another extension of Communion observances happening all over the world in hundreds of different settings on Sundays. You might mention this in your visit. You could even tell the person you're visiting something about the church service you shared with your congregation that week.

Remember that "body of Christ" refers in Scripture not only to Christ's body on the cross but also to the spiritual body of Christ, his church in the world today.

With this in mind, consider *sharing* in Communion with the person you're visiting instead of simply *serving* him or her the elements. Partake along with them to demonstrate the connection you share with them in Christ's body on earth.

Focus on the Cross

You may have made other sick or shut-in calls, but this one is unlike any other. You have a singular reason to make this visit.

This is more than a general encouraging visit. You want to do more than simply inspire. As is true with every Communion service in any setting, your goal here is to remember the fact and the purpose of the sacrifice of Jesus at Calvary.

This means you should bring more than a general devotional thought and offer more than a simple prayer of thanks for the day and request for healing and comfort for the person you're visiting. You may include any of those, of course, but don't leave out the significance of the shed blood and broken body represented by the common elements you are serving.

With this in mind, here are some Scripture suggestions and prayer prompts that could be especially meaningful for the person you'll visit at the hospital, nursing home, or sickbed:

Scripture to share: Romans 5:1-8

Therefore, since we have been justified through faith, we have peace with God through our Lord Jesus Christ, through whom we have gained access by faith into this grace in which we now stand. And we boast in the hope of the glory of God. Not only so, but we also glory in our sufferings, because we know that suffering produces perseverance; perseverance, character; and character, hope. And hope does not put us to shame, because God's love has been poured out into our hearts through the Holy Spirit, who has been given to us.

You see, at just the right time, when we were still powerless, Christ died for the ungodly. Very rarely will anyone die for a righteous person, though for a good person someone might possibly dare to die. But God demonstrates his own love for us in this: While we were still sinners, Christ died for us.

Prayer prompt: We thank you, God, for reminding us of the sufferings of Jesus because we know his sufferings allow him to identify with our sufferings in this moment. We know our ultimate peace is with you for eternity and is not limited by the physical health we are experiencing just now. We ask you to strengthen our hope because we've focused on the sacrifice of Jesus today.

Scripture to share: 2 Corinthians 1:3-4

Praise be to the God and Father of our Lord Jesus Christ, the Father of compassion and the God of all comfort, who comforts us in all our troubles, so that we can comfort those in any trouble with the comfort we ourselves receive from God.

Prayer prompt: Dear God of all comfort, we come to you for the comfort only you can provide, guaranteed for us by your lavish love and demonstrated for us in the remarkable sacrifice of Jesus.

Scripture to share: Galatians 2:20

I have been crucified with Christ and I no longer live, but Christ lives in me. The life I now live in the body, I live by faith in the Son of God, who loved me and gave himself for me.

Prayer prompt: With the apostle, we will affirm, dear God, that the life we live in our bodies continues only by your grace and your perfect will. Our faith in you is rooted in the sacrifice and resurrection of Jesus, and we thank you for the opportunity to remember both again today.

Scripture to share: Ephesians 1:7-10

In him we have redemption through his blood, the forgiveness of sins, in accordance with the riches of God's grace that he lavished on us. With all wisdom and understanding, he made known to us the mystery of his will according to his good pleasure, which he purposed in Christ, to be put into effect when the times reach their fulfillment—to bring unity to all things in heaven and on earth under Christ.

Prayer prompt: Even as we seek your grace for ourselves in this particular moment, dear God, we acknowledge your grace that gives every believer hope for eternity. Help us to revel in your lavish love even as we seek your helping hand for the days just ahead of us.

Scripture to share: Titus 2:11-14

For the grace of God has appeared that offers salvation to all people. It teaches us to say "No" to ungodliness and worldly passions, and to live self-controlled, upright and godly lives in this present age, while we wait for the blessed hope—the appearing of the glory of our great God and Savior, Jesus Christ, who gave himself for us to redeem us from all wickedness and to purify for himself a people that are his very own, eager to do what is good.

Prayer prompt: Dear Lord, we anticipate a glorious future as we celebrate the singular sacrifice of Jesus in a long-ago past. We seek the redemption and purification promised in your Word and made possible by the sacrifice of Jesus.

Scripture to share: Hebrews 12:1-3

Therefore, since we are surrounded by such a great cloud of witnesses, let us throw off everything that hinders and the sin that so easily entangles. And let us run with perseverance the race marked out for us, fixing our eyes on Jesus, the pioneer and perfecter of faith. For the joy set before him he endured the cross, scorning its shame, and sat down at the right hand of the throne of God. Consider him who endured such opposition from sinners, so that you will not grow weary and lose heart.

Prayer prompt: Lord, we confess that we're tempted to grow weary. The realities of this life are sometimes close to overwhelming. Thank you for reminding us that Jesus endured a tragic reality to provide us a hope-filled future.

Scripture to share: Hebrews 13:20-21

Now may the God of peace, who through the blood of the eternal covenant brought back from the dead our Lord Jesus, that great Shepherd of the sheep, equip you with everything good for doing his will, and may he work in us what is pleasing to him, through Jesus Christ, to whom be glory for ever and ever. Amen.

Prayer prompt: Quote this benediction as-is, directly from Scripture.

8 SCRIPTURES AND MEDITATION PROMPTS FOR PARTICULAR OCCASIONS

A few sentences under each of these Scriptures can guide your thoughts as you prepare a Communion meditation for a special service or unique occasion. Such as:

At a wedding
Ephesians 5:25-27

Husbands, love your wives, just as Christ loved the church and gave himself up for her to make her holy, cleansing her by the washing with water through the word, and to present her to himself as a radiant church, without stain or wrinkle or any other blemish, but holy and blameless.

"Radiant . . . without stain or wrinkle, or any other blemish." This is a picture of the bride who walked down the aisle today. This is the vision of the church God created by the sacrifice of his Son. As we celebrate this wedding, we also celebrate the new creation God has made of all of us who submit to the sacrifice of Jesus.

At a missionary send-off
Matthew 10:37-39

"Anyone who loves their father or mother more than me is not worthy of me; anyone who loves their son or daughter more than

me is not worthy of me. Whoever does not take up their cross and follow me is not worthy of me. Whoever finds their life will lose it, and whoever loses their life for my sake will find it."

As we commission this person (this team) (this couple) (this group) to sacrificial service in a challenging field, we remember they are doing so in obedience to the Lord's admonition: "Whoever finds their life will lose it, and whoever loses their life for my sake will find it." Imitating the selflessness of Jesus, who took up his cross, they are setting an example for each of us to consider as we remember his sacrifice today.

At a pastor ordination
1 Corinthians 2:1-5

And so it was with me, brothers and sisters. When I came to you, I did not come with eloquence or human wisdom as I proclaimed to you the testimony about God. For I resolved to know nothing while I was with you except Jesus Christ and him crucified. I came to you in weakness with great fear and trembling. My message and my preaching were not with wise and persuasive words, but with a demonstration of the Spirit's power, so that your faith might not rest on human wisdom, but on God's power.

Many around us are obsessed with the power of a good education. And while we will not deny what education offers, we must hear the words from one of the best-educated men of his time. His preaching focused on just one simple reality: the unique power of

Jesus' sacrifice on the cross to set our lives aright. This is what we remember today, even as we set aside one more servant to preach this truth for their lifetime.

At a baptism
Romans 6:1-4

What shall we say, then? Shall we go on sinning so that grace may increase? By no means! We are those who have died to sin; how can we live in it any longer? Or don't you know that all of us who were baptized into Christ Jesus were baptized into his death? We were therefore buried with him through baptism into death in order that, just as Christ was raised from the dead through the glory of the Father, we too may live a new life.

Baptism pictures the heart of the gospel, the burial and the resurrection of Christ. Our celebration of Communion reminds us of the power in the picture; Christ's death gives us the hope that our sins are covered by the saving shield of his blood.

At a funeral
Hebrews 12:1-3

Therefore, since we are surrounded by such a great cloud of witnesses, let us throw off everything that hinders and the sin that so easily entangles. And let us run with perseverance the race marked out for us, fixing our eyes on Jesus, the pioneer and perfecter of faith. For the joy set before him he endured the cross, scorning its shame, and sat down at the right hand of the throne of God. Consider him who endured such opposition from sinners, so that you will not grow weary and lose heart.

"For the joy set before him he endured the cross." What possible joy could Jesus have anticipated that would allow him to submit to the unimaginable agony of Calvary? One answer is this: He knew his sacrifice was only the prelude to his resurrection. And every believer today endures the sickness and sadness of this life, remembering it is only the first act of an eternal drama whose climax is that believer's resurrection to an eternal existence with the One who makes that hope possible.

9 SIX COMMUNION MEDITATIONS FOR SPECIAL DAYS

*W*hen asked to deliver a meditation on or close to a holiday, some may tend to wander away from the central message of the cross as they think about the event on the calendar. Here are meditations for some of these special days. You may adapt some of them for use anytime. Meanwhile, use them as prods to help you think about how the significance of the holiday can be acknowledged in the light of Christ's sacrifice.

New Year: Truly Something New

Have you ever asked yourself why people celebrate New Year's? Why the fireworks, the crowd, the revelry, the cheers, the toasts?

Some, I suppose, are just up for any occasion to party.

Maybe some, given all the challenges of this life, are just glad they made it through another year.

Some contribute to the rhetoric about new beginnings, new opportunities, a fresh start. It's an appealing idea for all of us because each of us has some wrong choice, bad decision, or unfortunate mistake whose effects they can't shake off. For some, our lives are like a smartphone junked up with unused apps, inaccurate contacts, unread emails, and unwanted viruses, and we'd like just to trade in what we're carrying around and start with all new.

Today we're celebrating the fact that "all new" is possible. Jesus told his followers on the night he instituted the Lord's Supper that he'd come to establish a new covenant between humans and God (Luke 22:20). This was to be an agreement based not on earning goodness by following the Law but on reveling in grace available to all through the blood of Jesus.

"If anyone is in Christ," Paul wrote the Corinthian church, "the new creation has come: The old has gone, the new is here!" (2 Corinthians 5:17).

This means all those poor choices and embarrassing mistakes will not be chalked up against us. This means we can give up trying to be good enough and simply relax in the goodness of God. This means the world's systems of rules-keeping and point-counting need not determine the way we live our lives. This means Christians living by the New Covenant are free from all of that. Jesus asked us to remember that every time we gather for the Lord's Supper.

This is why we celebrate this morning. And it's a celebration that won't need to wait till next January 1 for us to enjoy again. For us, everything's new! It's hard to imagine anything better.

Valentine's Day: Love Is All You Need

"Love Is All You Need" was the theme of a Beatles hit several decades ago and later the title of a 2012 romantic comedy produced in Denmark. I suppose many celebrating Valentine's Day this week would agree with the assertion. Indeed, our popular culture works to convince us that love is the ultimate value, our highest purpose.

"Do what you love," we tell middle adults wondering about their career choices.

"But I love her," proclaims the divorcing husband, as if that sentence alone justifies his betrayal of his wife and children.

Christians have the opportunity to look more seriously at love, to contemplate the sacrifice and suffering and sometimes just the slog of love when we look at the life of Jesus, "Who, being in very nature God, did not consider equality with God something to be used to his own advantage; rather, he made himself nothing by taking the very nature of a servant." There is no better example of love.

We might wonder how many proclaiming love this Valentine's Day are doing so with a commitment to subjugate themselves in service to the object of their affection. Do we love someone who rejects us? Do we love someone who doesn't appreciate us? Do we love someone requiring painful sacrifice? Jesus did.

"And being found in appearance as a man, he humbled himself by becoming obedient to death— even death on a cross!" (Philippians 2:6-8).

Love in human relationships is not a simple thing, more complicated, indeed, than we have time to analyze at this time in our worship. And besides that, this isn't the place.

This is the place to focus on the purest example of love the world has seen, when the divine took on humanity, not to wield superpower (although he had all power), not to impress with his knowledge (although his understanding was broader and more complete than we can fathom), but to serve us. And save us. And love us. And invite us to love too. "By this everyone will know that you are my disciples," he said, "if you love one another" (John 13:35).

And so, as we partake today, we remember love, and we thank God for the love Jesus demonstrated by his life and his sacrificial death.

Easter: Twin Events

Some might wonder why we would pause to talk about death on a day we're supposed to be celebrating new life. But the fact is that the death of Christ gives the reason to celebrate the resurrection of Christ. The crucifixion and the resurrection are twin events with a singular purpose, to make possible salvation from sin for all who accept the Jesus who experienced them both.

If Jesus had died a natural death, like Lazarus, and been miraculously raised from the dead, that event would have given us reason to believe in God, but it would tell us nothing about Jesus. We have no reason to worship Lazarus.

If Jesus had died at the government's hand, ending a remarkable teaching and healing career, and was buried in a tomb visited by those who loved him, some of them probably would have continued to follow him. But his story would have sunk into the musty pages of history like that of so many other remarkable cause-bearers through history.

But Jesus was no ordinary martyr, and his was not a manmade cause or message. Speaking of his followers, Jesus said, "I have come that they may have life, and have it to the full" (John 10:10). This is a supernatural life, given by the one whose death made it possible for ordinary human beings.

Paul put it this way in his letter to the Corinthian church: "Christ has indeed been raised from the dead, the firstfruits of those who have fallen asleep. For since death came through a man, the resurrection of the dead comes also through a man. For as in Adam all die, so in Christ all will be made alive" (1 Corinthians 15:20-22).

The accomplishment in the death of Jesus is proven by the resurrection of Jesus. In a way, we celebrate both every time we worship, and no less on Easter Sunday.

And so today we celebrate—the death of God's Son who knew no sin, and the resurrection of God's Son who came to spare us from the sting of death. Hallelujah! What a Savior!

Patriotic Holidays: More Than a Hero

When we think of national heroes—soldiers who stormed into battle against overwhelming odds, sailors who fought with the fear that their ships could be blown out of the sea, marines who undertook desperate missions and ignored peril to bring back their own fallen comrades—when we think of those who fought and died to secure our freedom, sometimes we're tempted to put Jesus in the same category.

But without taking away any honor due our national heroes, we must at this moment acknowledge that Jesus was more and accomplished more than anyone who has fought on any battlefield.

When we think of our fallen heroes, we remember those who died to secure a temporary peace. But Jesus died to make possible a peace that passes understanding (Philippians 4:7).

Our heroes died to protect political freedom. Jesus died to give us freedom from spiritual guilt and emotional shame (Romans 10:11).

Our many heroes died for some people, the population of their country. Jesus, just Jesus alone, died for all people in all places at all times (Romans 5:19).

Our heroes return to their homeland to reunite with family and friends. Jesus returned to the amazement of a small band of disciples but lives today in eternal glory where someday every knee will bow and every voice will be raised to call him Lord (Philippians 2:9-11).

Our heroes won some battles but lost some others. Jesus overcame the ultimate evil, Satan himself, and lives in a victory that every one of his followers can claim (1 Corinthians 15:57).

We decorate the graves of our heroes. We remember the empty tomb of Jesus.

Our heroes are tasked with inspiring future generations and raising up new heroes to follow in their footsteps. Jesus promised a Comforter, the Holy Spirit, who is immediately available to everyone who will follow him (John 14:15-17).

We may not be wrong to call Jesus a hero. But in the same breath, we must acknowledge that he is more. He is King of kings and Lord of lords (1 Timothy 6:15), and he accomplished at the cross what everyone needs and only he could provide.

We celebrate Jesus today more than a hero remembered on one holiday; our Savior is worshipped every time we gather in his name.

Thanksgiving: Taste and See

Sometimes we tend to take for granted the blessings in life for which we ought to be most grateful. The love of our spouses, the joy we find in our children, the security that's ours because of our jobs, our freedom to pursue life as we wish, our health, our full pantries, our safe homes.

Sometimes we appreciate any of these most only after we have begun to lose them.

But the gift for which we can be most grateful is the one we will not lose with time or changing circumstances, the salvation granted us through the sacrificial death of our Lord Jesus on the cross. And like all the other "good and perfect gifts" showered down on us from the Father above (James 1:17), we may take this salvation for granted.

Some of us have a habit of ignoring what should cause us gratitude. We may kiss our spouse goodnight every bedtime without thinking about the passion that drew us together when we were first married. We may order from an impressive menu without stopping to remember the days when we couldn't afford to eat out at all. And we may go through the motions of worship without giving ourselves time to be awestruck again by what Christ really did for us.

This has been true from the beginning. Paul felt compelled to remind the early Roman Christians this way: "But thanks be to God that, though you used to be slaves to sin, you have come to obey from your heart the pattern of teaching that has now claimed your allegiance" (Romans 6:17). This morning as we meet at this table, let us thank God for our new allegiance.

He wrote the Corinthians, "The sting of death is sin, and the power of sin is the law. But thanks be to God! He gives us the victory through our Lord Jesus Christ" (1 Corinthians 15:56-57). People all around us are scurrying in fear of death or what comes afterward. Just this year, all of us know people plunged into despair because of a separation caused by the death of someone they love. Today we thank God that Christ's death and resurrection have removed that sting for us.

As we pause to drink from the cup and eat from the loaf, let us taste and see the goodness of our Lord for giving us what we need most. And let us be thankful.

Christmas: Swaddling Clothes

The Sight and Sound Theatres production *Jesus* makes a memorable comparison between the birth of Jesus and his death. Across a giant stage, the audience sees two scenes unfolding. One shows Mary wrapping her newborn Jesus in cloths and placing him in a manger (Luke 2:7). But this happy scene is juxtaposed with Mary wrapping the blood-stained body of her crucified Son in a clean linen cloth provided by a wealthy Jewish believer, Joseph of Arimathea, who allowed the burial of Jesus in his own tomb (Matthew 27:57-59).

Jesus: He was born away from home in the lowliest of circumstances, kept warm and clean in a wrapping of simple cloth. Jesus: He was buried in a borrowed tomb, wrapped in donated linen after suffering an unjust death. The crying, cooing infant entered the world through a human womb to become the bleeding Savior who died in agony and was then buried in a donated tomb.

Since his birth, death, and resurrection became the centerpiece of history so many centuries ago, humankind has created myriad, elaborate trappings to accompany our celebrations. Merchandisers and romantics have devised all kinds of decorations and traditions surrounding both events.

Indeed, even for many Christians, finding moments to meditate on the reality of his birth may become almost impossible as we prepare for gift-giving, family meals, children's programs, and Christmas concerts.

When Easter comes, the empty tomb competes in the public eye with plastic eggs and bunny ears and shelves laden with too much chocolate, all demanding the attention of those who celebrate.

But at this moment, at this table, we have the opportunity to strip away all those manmade conventions and focus on the simple story that is the reason for our hope and the motivator for our lives.

Christ, the Lord of the universe, came as a human being to show us what God is really like and to identify with all the toil and trouble that is our daily lot. This fragile baby became a towering figure of a man who willingly submitted to the taunts and trials of a criminal's execution just to accomplish for us what we could not do on our own.

We remember Easter as we celebrate Christmas, and in the middle of both, we hold up the cross. We eat the fruit of the vine and share the broken loaf today because we realize they symbolize the sacrifice of why Christ was born.

10 TWO EXTENDED COMMUNION SERVICE OUTLINES

*T*he following Communion outlines offer you a couple longer service options that can be applied in a variety of settings. Be it at a retreat, in a small group, or during a special worship or prayer service when you're free to spend more than the usual amount of time celebrating Communion.

Outline 1: Come Home

In a retreat setting, distribute slips of paper and ask volunteers to complete this sentence, "When I think of home, I think of . . . ." Collect the slips and read a few to the group.

In a church service, suggest several possible finishes to the sentence or collect a few from others ahead of time for you to read now.

Share this introduction with your group:

The Stolpersteine project, initiated by the German artist Gunter Denning in 1992, marks the homeplaces of displaced Jews and others who were taken from their homes and imprisoned or exterminated by Nazi Germany almost a century ago. Each Stolperstein (literally, "stumbling block") is a 3.9-inch square concrete block bearing a brass plate engraved with the names and dates of victims of this Holocaust. Each block is placed in front of the last known address or workplace of those named on its plate. The Stolpersteine commemorate for the world the homes of those who lost them.

Those who survived have shared how important it is to them to have these memorials. "The world may remember so much that we lost," they have said. "But many forget how devastating it is that our homes were taken, and now we have no place beckoning us home. Our homes were eliminated."

All this reminds us that home is a vital place, a vital concept for all of us. Jesus told his disciples that he was leaving earth to prepare a home for them. And we believe we will have an eternal home with him also. Today, he is beckoning you to look toward that home.

So, just now, pretend that Jesus is standing before us with outstretched hand, in an invitation for you and for me. Close your eyes and listen to a new version of an old hymn,[4] and consider, "What does it mean to me that Jesus is inviting me home?"

---

4   Play a slow and warm rendition of a familiar hymn. By way of example, consider something like Carrie Underwood's version of "Just as I Am," or an arrangement of it by another artist.

In interludes between the stanzas, ask one or two readers to read the following verses. Or read them to introduce the song.

Reader One: Come to me, all you who are weary and burdened, and I will give you rest. Take my yoke upon you and learn from me, for I am gentle and humble in heart, and you will find rest for your souls. For my yoke is easy and my burden is light (Matthew 11:28-30).

Reader Two: Here I am! I stand at the door and knock. If anyone hears my voice and opens the door, I will come in and eat with that person, and they with me (Revelation 3:20).

After the song:

Reader Three: Just as I am, poor, wretched, blind;
                 Sight, riches, healing of the mind,
                 Yea, all I need in Thee to find,
                 O Lamb of God, I come, I come.

Group sings: *Just as I am, without one plea*
                 But that Thy blood was shed for me,
                 And that Thou bidd'st me come to Thee,
                 O Lamb of God, I come, I come.

Reader Four: For you know that it was not with perishable things such as silver or gold that you were redeemed from the empty way of life handed down to you from your ancestors, but with the precious blood of Christ, a lamb without blemish or defect (1 Peter 1:18-19).

Group sings: *Just as I am, and waiting not*
To rid my soul of one dark blot,
To Thee whose blood can cleanse each spot,
O Lamb of God, I come, I come.

Reader Five: "Come now, let us settle the matter," says the LORD. "Though your sins are like scarlet, they shall be as white as snow; though they are red as crimson, they shall be like wool" (Isaiah 1:18).

Group sings: *Just as I am, though tossed about*
With many a conflict, many a doubt,
Fightings within, and fears without,
O Lamb of God, I come, I come.

Reader Six: You see, at just the right time, when we were still powerless, Christ died for the ungodly. Very rarely will anyone die for a righteous person, though for a good person someone might possibly dare to die. But God demonstrates his own love for us in this: While we were still sinners, Christ died for us (Romans 5:6-8).

Group sings: *Just as I am, Thou wilt receive,*
                Wilt welcome, pardon, cleanse, relieve;
                Because Thy promise I believe,
                O Lamb of God, I come, I come.

Reader Seven: If anyone is in Christ, the new creation has come: The old has gone, the new is here! All this is from God, who reconciled us to himself through Christ and gave us the ministry of reconciliation: that God was reconciling the world to himself in Christ, not counting people's sins against them. . . . God made him who had no sin to be sin for us, so that in him we might become the righteousness of God (2 Corinthians 5:17-19, 21).

Prayer prompt before receiving Communion:

> "Thank you, God, for the invitation of Jesus to come to him and to meet him at this table of remembrance. While we wait for and look forward to that eternal home before you with him, help us to rest at this temporary dwelling place, a waystation that gives us security now with the promise of home at last for eternity with you someday. We know that the blood of Jesus sacrificed at Calvary has opened the door to this home, and we thank you."

Partake of Communion

Offer a closing prayer of gratitude

Outline 2: My Soul, My Life, My All

Distribute or project the following responsive reading, taken from 1 Corinthians 11:23-26; Isaiah 53:4-6; and 2 Corinthians 5:17-21.

Leader: The Lord Jesus, on the night he was betrayed, took bread, and when he had given thanks, he broke it and said,

Men: "This is my body, which is for you; do this in remembrance of me."

Leader: In the same way, after supper he took the cup, saying,

Men: "This cup is the new covenant in my blood; do this, whenever you drink it, in remembrance of me."

Leader: For whenever you eat this bread and drink this cup,

Women: you proclaim the Lord's death until he comes.

Congregation or group sings the first two stanzas of "When I Survey the Wondrous Cross" by Isaac Watts

Leader: Surely he took up our pain and bore
                 our suffering,

Women: yet we considered him punished by
                 God, stricken by him, and afflicted.

Leader: But   he   was   pierced   for   our
                 transgressions,

Men: he was crushed for our iniquities;

Leader: the punishment that brought us peace
                 was on him,

Women: and by his wounds we are healed.

Leader: We all, like sheep, have gone astray,
                 each of us has turned to our own way;

EVERYONE: and the LORD has laid on him the
                 iniquity of us all.

Sing Stanza 3 of "When I Survey the Wondrous Cross"

Prayers of thanks for the sacrifice of Jesus

*Recruit several to pray. In a smaller group, you may ask for
voluntary sentence prayers.*

Partaking of the Elements

Option: invite participants to come to one or more stations to partake.

Leader:
> If anyone is in Christ, the new creation has come: The old has gone, the new is here!

Women:
> All this is from God, who reconciled us to himself through Christ and gave us the ministry of reconciliation:

Men:
> that God was reconciling the world to himself in Christ, not counting people's sins against them.

Women:
> And he has committed to us the message of reconciliation.

Leader:
> We are therefore Christ's ambassadors, as though God were making his appeal through us. We implore you on Christ's behalf: Be reconciled to God.

EVERYONE:
> God made him who had no sin to be sin for us, so that in him we might become the righteousness of God.

To close, sing stanza 4 of "When I Survey the Wondrous Cross"

About the Contributors

Author
Mark A. Taylor spent most of his career in Christian publishing, finishing with his stint as publisher and editor of *Christian Standard* magazine. In retirement, he continues to pursue a variety of teaching, editing, and writing opportunities, including his latest project, *Unchosen Journey: A Caregiver's Walk with Alzheimer's* (www.unchosenjourney.com). He and his wife, Evelyn, live north of Cincinnati, Ohio.

General Editor
Matthew Lockhart spent more than twenty-five years serving in a variety of editorial and leadership roles in Christian publishing at Serendipity House, Group, and Standard/David C. Cook. With a penchant for book series development, he enjoys helping to create Kingdom-focused resources like the *ChurchLeaders Pastoral Pocket Guides*.